WRITE *Your* HEART OUT

Colorful Crow Publishing
Calhoun, GA
ColorfulCrowPublishing.com

ISBN: 978-1-964271-36-1

Printing 1: November 2025

Printed in the United States of America

WRITE *Your* HEART OUT

A 52-WEEK REFLECTIVE WRITING JOURNAL

By Vickie McEntire

Colorful Crow Publishing
Calhoun, Georgia

Welcome!

Dear Writer,

Welcome to *Write Your Heart Out*.

This journal is your companion for the next 52 weeks — a space to slow down, breathe, and listen to your own voice.

Each week, you'll find a prompt to guide you, but the heart of this book is yours. Use the prompts as springboards, or wander wherever your writing takes you.

There are no rules here, only invitations.

Write bravely.

Write gently.

Write your heart out.

With gratitude and admiration,

Vickie McEntire

How to Use This Journal

• Set aside 15-20 minutes once a week.

• Start with the week's prompt, or choose one from the list at the front.

• Let the words flow — don't edit yourself.

• At the end of each quarter, use the reflection pages to notice what themes or patterns are emerging.

• Most importantly: enjoy the act of writing.

Your Year of

1. What is your earliest memory that still shapes you today?
2. Write about a time when you felt truly at peace.
3. What personal strength do you overlook in yourself?
4. Reflect on a moment of failure that taught you something vital.
5. What does "home" mean to you now?
6. Describe a habit that quietly sustains you.
7. Write about a turning point in your life.
8. When do you feel most like yourself?
9. Recall a time when silence spoke louder than words.
10. What do you need to forgive yourself for?
11. Describe a part of your daily routine that feels sacred.
12. Write about an object you've kept for years — what story does it hold?
13. What does "rest" look like for you right now?
14. Who has shaped your life the most, and how?
15. Recall a conversation you'll never forget.
16. Write about a friendship that changed you.
17. How do you want to be remembered by those closest to you?
18. What role does family play in your story?
19. Write about a time you felt deeply understood.
20. Reflect on someone you admire — what qualities do they carry?
21. What relationship has been your greatest teacher?
22. How do you express love? How do you receive it?
23. Write about a goodbye that still lingers.
24. Recall a moment when laughter healed something in you.
25. What tradition or ritual connects you to others?
26. Who do you need to thank, and why?

Reflection Prompts

27. Describe a place in nature that feels like refuge.

28. What season best reflects your spirit, and why?

29. Reflect on a journey that opened your eyes.

30. Write about a book, song, or piece of art that changed you.

31. When was the last time you felt awe?

32. What lesson has travel taught you?

33. How do you find beauty in ordinary things?

34. Write about the smell, sound, or taste that carries memory.

35. Recall a time when the natural world spoke to you.

36. What does your community give you, and what do you give back?

37. Reflect on how the world has changed in your lifetime.

38. Write about a moment when you witnessed kindness.

39. Where do you see hope in the world around you?

40. What is the most important lesson you want to pass on?

41. Write about a dream you still hold.

42. How has your idea of success shifted over time?

43. Reflect on a time when you were braver than you knew.

44. What unfinished story do you want to keep writing?

45. Write about an obstacle you overcame.

46. What advice would your younger self give you now?

47. What advice would you give your younger self?

48. How do you want your life to feel five years from now?

49. What legacy do you hope to leave behind?

50. Write about the gifts you've been given that can't be measured.

51. What brings you the deepest sense of meaning?

52. Reflect on the year of journaling: What surprised you? What changed in you?

What is your earliest memory that still shapes you today?

_____

_____

_____

_____

_____

_____

_____

_____

_____

_____

_____

_____

_____

_____

_____

_____

_____

_____

_____

_____

_____

_____

_____

Write about a time when you felt truly at peace.

_____

_____

_____

_____

_____

_____

_____

_____

_____

_____

_____

_____

_____

_____

_____

_____

_____

_____

_____

_____

_____

_____

_____

_____

_____

What personal strength do you overlook in yourself?

Reflect on a moment of failure that taught you something vital.

Week 4

What does "home" mean to you now?

Describe a habit that quietly sustains you.

Week 6

Write about a turning point in your life.

Week 7

When do you feel most like yourself?

Week 8

Recall a time when silence spoke louder than words.

What do you need to forgive yourself for?

Week 10

Describe a part of your daily routine that feels sacred.

Week 11

Write about an object you've kept for years — what story does it hold?

Week 12

What does "rest" look like for you right now?

"We write to taste life twice, in the moment
and in retrospection."

—*Anaïs Nin*

At the end of this season, pause and look back over your writing journey. Use these questions to deepen your reflection:

- **What surprised you most in your writing this season?**
- **What patterns or themes keep showing up in your reflections?**
- **Which prompt was the most meaningful for you, and why?**
- **Where have you noticed growth or change in yourself?**
- **What questions do you want to carry forward into the next season?**

_____

_____

_____

_____

_____

_____

_____

_____

_____

_____

_____

_____

_____

_____

_____

_____

Quarterly Reflection

Who has shaped your life the most, and how?

Week 14

Recall a conversation you'll never forget.

_____

_____

_____

_____

_____

_____

_____

_____

_____

_____

_____

_____

_____

_____

_____

_____

_____

_____

_____

_____

_____

_____

_____

_____

Write about a friendship that changed you.

How do you want to be remembered by those closest to you?

What role does family play in your story?

Week 18

Write about a time you felt deeply understood.

Week 19

Reflect on someone you admire — what qualities do they carry?

What relationship has been your greatest teacher?

_____

_____

_____

_____

_____

_____

_____

_____

_____

_____

_____

_____

_____

_____

_____

_____

_____

_____

_____

_____

_____

How do you express love? How do you receive it?

Write about a goodbye that still lingers.

Recall a moment when laughter healed something in you.

Week 24

What tradition or ritual connects you to others?

Who do you need to thank, and why?

"Preserve your memories, keep them well, what you forget you can never retell."

— *Louisa May Alcott*

At the end of this season, pause and look back over your writing journey. Use these questions to deepen your reflection:

- **What surprised you most in your writing this season?**
- **What patterns or themes keep showing up in your reflections?**
- **Which prompt was the most meaningful for you, and why?**
- **Where have you noticed growth or change in yourself?**
- **What questions do you want to carry forward into the next season?**

_____

_____

_____

_____

_____

_____

_____

_____

_____

_____

_____

_____

_____

_____

_____

Quarterly Reflection

Describe a place in nature that feels like refuge.

What season best reflects your spirit, and why?

Reflect on a journey that opened your eyes.

Week 29

Write about a book, song, or piece of art that changed you.

Week 30

When was the last time you felt awe?

What lesson has travel taught you?

How do you find beauty in ordinary things?

Write about the smell, sound, or taste that carries memory.

Recall a time when the natural world spoke to you.

What does your community give you, and what do you give back?

Reflect on how the world has changed in your lifetime.

Write about a moment when you witnessed kindness.

Where do you see hope in the world around you?

"I write entirely to find out what I'm thinking, what I'm looking at, what I see and what it means."

— *Joan Didion*

At the end of this season, pause and look back over your writing journey. Use these questions to deepen your reflection:

- **What surprised you most in your writing this season?**
- **What patterns or themes keep showing up in your reflections?**
- **Which prompt was the most meaningful for you, and why?**
- **Where have you noticed growth or change in yourself?**
- **What questions do you want to carry forward into the next season?**

_____

_____

_____

_____

_____

_____

_____

_____

_____

_____

_____

_____

_____

_____

_____

_____

Quarterly Reflection

What is the most important lesson you want to pass on?

Write about a dream you still hold.

How has your idea of success shifted over time?

Week 42

Reflect on a time when you were braver than you knew.

What unfinished story do you want to keep writing?

Write about an obstacle you overcame.

What advice would your younger self give you now?

What advice would you give your younger self?

How do you want your life to feel five years from now?

What legacy do you hope to leave behind?

Write about the gifts you've been given that can't be measured.

What brings you the deepest sense of meaning?

Reflect on the year of journaling: What surprised or changed you?

Week 52

"Keep a notebook. Travel with it, eat with it, sleep with it. Slap into it every stray thought that flutters up into your brain. Cheap paper is less perishable than gray matter. And lead pencil markings endure longer than memory."

— *Jack London*

At the end of this season, pause and look back over your writing journey. Use these questions to deepen your reflection:

- **What surprised you most in your writing this season?**
- **What patterns or themes keep showing up in your reflections?**
- **Which prompt was the most meaningful for you, and why?**
- **Where have you noticed growth or change in yourself?**
- **What questions do you want to carry forward into the next season?**

_____

_____

_____

_____

_____

_____

_____

_____

_____

_____

_____

_____

_____

_____

_____

_____

_____

Quarterly Reflection

Congratulations!

Dear Writer,

Think about what you've done here. For 52 weeks, you showed up for yourself. You made space for your thoughts when the world demanded your attention elsewhere. You wrote through the ordinary weeks and the extraordinary ones, and in doing so, you recorded conversations with your truest self.

Take a few minutes to savor and celebrate your achievement, and that's exactly what this is — *an achievement.* Eat a piece of chocolate. Buy yourself a shirt. Toast yourself with a glass of your favorite wine. Don't let this moment slip away without some form of commemoration.

But know this: The journey isn't over. It is just beginning. The habit you've built is a gift that will keep giving. I encourage you to keep writing your heart out. Keep going. Keep writing. Keep discovering.

Well done my friend! I am so proud of you.

With gratitude and admiration,